Origins

Danger in the Dark

Janet Foxley · Davide Ortu

Humphrey was a hippo. He lived with his mother and the other hippos in a cool lake in Africa. All day long Humphrey and the others lay happily in the lake.

Every night, the other hippos left the lake to look for tasty grass to eat.

Humphrey didn't want to go with them today. He didn't like walking.

"Come on, Humphrey," said his mother. "There isn't enough grass here by the lake. We need to go and find the long, clean grass."

"I'm not hungry," said Humphrey, sitting down.

"You won't like staying at the lake on your own, Humphrey. It's very dark and you will get hungry before long," said Mum.
"I WILL NOT!" said Humphrey.

"There are crocodiles in the lake. If you're by yourself they might try to eat you," said Mum.

Humphrey laughed. She often tried to frighten him with stories of crocodiles. "I'm not stupid," he said. "I don't believe in crocodiles."

"Nothing frightens me, Mum!" said Humphrey. "Especially not the dark."

Mum sighed. She went off with the other hippos to look for grass.

Humphrey liked to pretend he was brave, but really he *was* afraid of the dark. He tried shutting his eyes so he couldn't see the dark. But the dark sounded even worse than it looked. Humphrey wished he could shut his ears, so that he couldn't hear the dark.

Humphrey was sure he could hear a hungry lion roaring ... a frightened animal howling ... and footsteps, coming closer!

Humphrey quickly moved back into the deep water of the lake.

Now that he felt safer, Humphrey realized he was hungry after all. He didn't want to leave the lake on his own, though. The noises from the land were too scary.

Just then he heard a different noise – a noise he knew. It was a splashing noise. "Good!" thought Humphrey. "There must be more hippos splashing about on the far side of the lake. I'll go and ask them where I can find some food."

Humphrey hadn't swum far when he found someone to talk to. That someone was small, green and bumpy.

His name was Rocco. He didn't look much like a hippo. He was catching fish to eat. Humphrey said, "Hello! Please can I share your supper?"

"No, because hippos don't eat fish," said Rocco. "Fish are crocodile food – and so are hippos."

"C ... crocodile?" said Humphrey. A shiver ran down his back. "Crocodiles aren't real, are they?"

Rocco laughed. "I'm real, aren't I?"

"You're a *crocodile*?" Humphrey gasped. "But you couldn't eat me – you're smaller than I am!"

"*I* couldn't, no, but my father, Griff, could gobble you up easily," said Rocco, opening his mouth wide. "If I were you, I'd run away before he finds you."

Humphrey swam away as fast as he could. Just then, a thick cloud covered the moon. It was so dark that Humphrey soon got lost.
"I don't like the dark," thought Humphrey.

Just then Humphrey saw an animal he knew. It was Ethel, an aardvark who often came to drink at the lake. "Perhaps Ethel can tell me the way home," thought Humphrey.

But someone else had seen Ethel, too. Someone was creeping up on her, someone as big as a tree trunk with a great mouth full of sharp teeth. Griff!

"Ethel hasn't seen him!" Humphrey thought. "If I warn her though, Griff will see *me*!"

He held his breath and lay as still as a rock. Griff crept closer ...

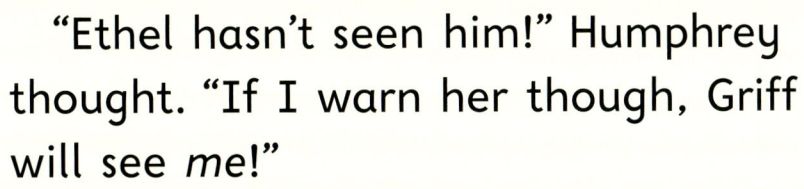

"I can't do it!" thought Humphrey. "I can't just hide and let Griff eat Ethel!"
"Run, Ethel!" Humphrey shouted.
Ethel ran.

Griff turned and looked at Humphrey. For the first time in his life, Humphrey ran, too. He followed Ethel as fast as he could.

At last Ethel reached a small cave and ran inside. Humphrey rushed after her. His heart was pounding.

Safe at last!

"It's very dark in here, but I don't mind!" Humphrey thought. "Sometimes, dark is good!"

Humphrey and Ethel hid until they heard Griff go back to the lake.

Now Humphrey had a great story to tell Mum when she came back. He wasn't afraid of the *dark* any more, but he definitely *was* scared of crocodiles!